Holy Week in Seville

Editorial Everest would like to thank you for purchasing this book. It has been created by an extensive and complete publishing team made up of photographers, illustrators and authors specialised in the field of tourism, together with our modern cartography department. Everest guarantees that the contents of this work were completely up to date at the time of going to press, and we would like to invite you to send us any information that helps us to improve our publications, so that we may always offer QUALITY TOURISM.

QUALITY TOURISM WITH EVEREST

Please send your comments to:
Editorial Everest. Dpto. de Turismo
Apartado 339 - 24080 León (Spain)
Or e-mail them to us at turismo@everest.es

Editorial Management: Raquel López Varela

Editorial Coordination: Eva María Fernández and Esteban González

Text: Carlos Colón Perales

Photographs: José Antonio Zamora, Miguel Raurich, Gabriel M.ª Pou, Grupo ASA-24, Esteban González and Everest Archives

Cover design: Alfredo Anievas

Translation: Babyl Traducciones

No part of this book may be reproduced or processed by computer or transmitted by any means, electronic, mechanical, photocopying, registration or otherwise without the prior permission in writing of the Copyright holders.
All rights reserved, including the right of sale, hire, loan or any other way of making over the use of the copy.

© EDITORIAL EVEREST, S. A.
Carretera León-A Coruña, km 5 – LEÓN
ISBN: 84-241-0537-0
Legal deposit: LE. 708-2005
Printed in Spain

EDITORIAL EVERGRÁFICAS, S. L.
Carretera León-A Coruña, km 5
LEÓN (Spain)

HOLY WEEK IN SEVILLE

Holy Week or Semana Santa originates from an encounter between Seville and God, that is to say, between a belief, that of Christianity and a city, that of Seville, which are so deeply fused that it becomes difficult to distinguish the boundaries between religion and daily life. Where does it all start and finish, in the people of Seville's emotions, the sacred and the profane, the temple and the street, private lives and religious beings, their love and their devotion? The churches, thanks to the brotherhoods, put all their efforts throughout the year, into the glazed tiles which represent the sacred images in order that the faithful can pray when they are closed and in some way to consecrate and sanctify the profane places with their presence. By contrast, during Holy Week the street appears to encroach upon the temples to shelter the bustling and almost chaotic multitude of onlooker's and worshippers who appear every morning to see the *pasos*, or floats, whilst, by contrast, in the afternoons and evenings the streets and plazas become temples welcoming the long processional entourage escorting the sacred images on the portable altars of their floats, from the churches to the Cathedral.

HOLY WEEK IN SEVILLE

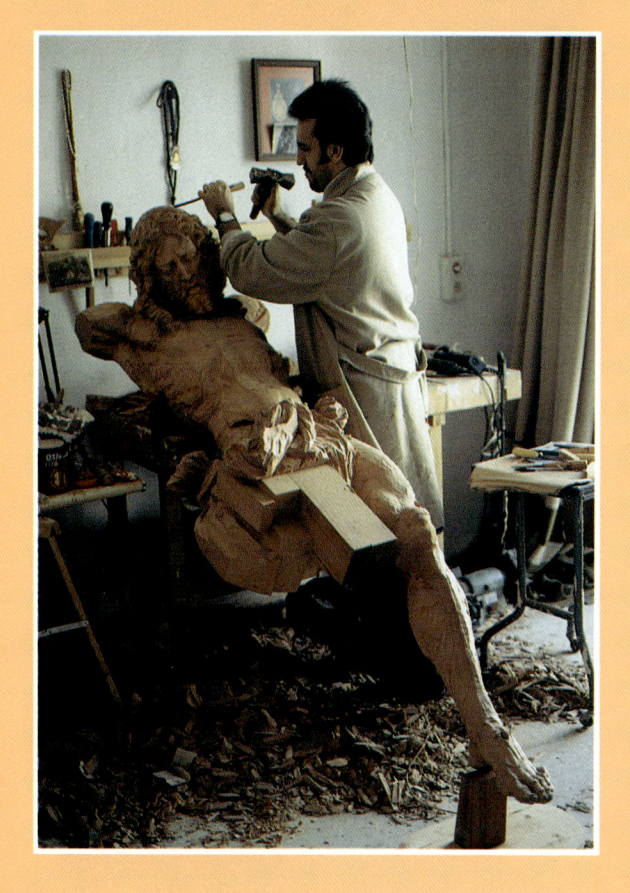

4

Traditional crafts associated with the Holy Week.

Anyone who passes through Seville any day of the year will not only see these beautiful glazed tiles with their sacred images on church façades and private houses; they will also see photographs in shops and bars and, if close to a Sevillian, they will likewise be seen in the album along with the mass of family photos, and in their houses. This custom is by no means limited to the traditional nor to the city's historic district: if you go to one of the large stores you will see them imprinted on the cash registers and should you visit a modern district, however distant it may be from the centre, you will see these photographs in shops and bars, as if they had never come out of the ancient districts organized around the parishes and the age old brotherhoods residing therein. Although Holy Week is essentially a baroque festival the most significant brotherhoods having been founded between the 15th and 17th century and the most spectacular and devout images sculptured in the 17th century, it doesn't end here, they have not ceased to create new associations in line with the city's growth and to sculpture new images on their behalf, as if the new districts have the need to manifest their link with the historic city and establish a base in this devotional land that is Seville, through the brotherhoods and their dedication to these images.

Nevertheless their exists aesthetic, historic and devotional hierarchies and it is not these new districts, to which Holy Week refers to as, the "colonies" which lived "subject to" the historic city; nor is it the brotherhoods, more recently, less numerous than their more illustrious predecessors. Seville, founded by Hercules, surrounded by Julius Cesar's walls and the seat of emperors Trajano and Adriano, is a Roman city; and Rome, when it conquered, converted the new towns to Roman.

"Azulejos" (Glazed tiles) Above, Gran Poder (God).
Below, Christ of Calvary

HOLY WEEK IN SEVILLE

6

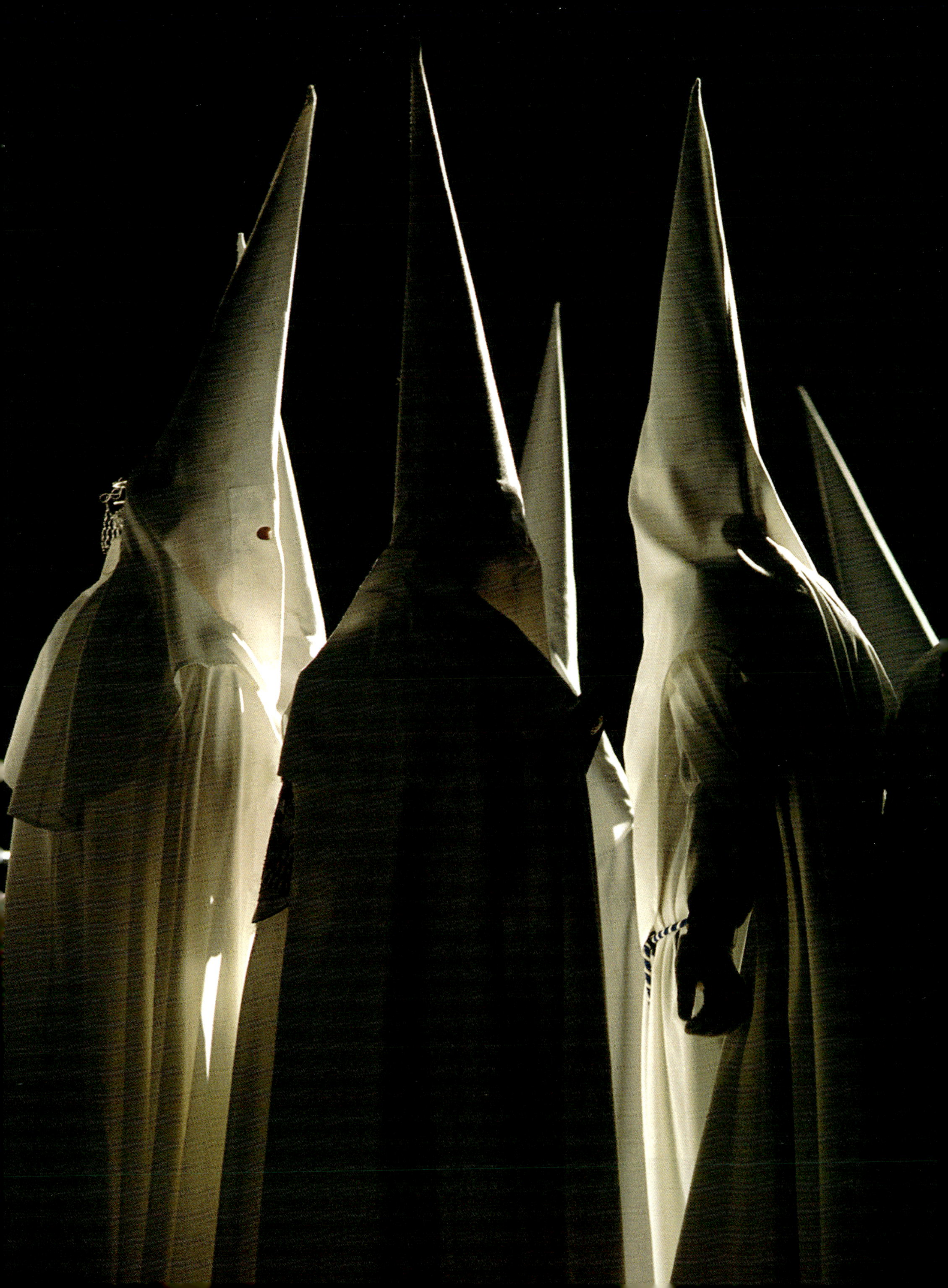

HOLY WEEK IN SEVILLE

Romanisation consisted of integrating the new lands with Rome, in place of imposing upon them a tyrannical and distant power condemned forever with foreign status. Seville was established in this way: continually taking possession of newly acquired lands from the end of the 19th century extending beyond the centuries old perimeter of its historic walls, the memory of which is preserved in the ring roads, those named Florida, María Auxiliadora, Capuchinos, Resolana, Torneo follow its original route and the large crossroads and wide stretches retain the names of the city's ancient *puertas* or gateways: such as the puertas de Jerez, de la Carne, de Carmona, del Osario, del Sol, de Córdoba or Real. What it is to be a Sevillian, so easy to recognise, yet so difficult to define without inviting clichés, is an invisible

Paso of La Borriquita on Palm Sunday.

Palm Sunday.

Above, Paso of the Brotherhood of the Star.

Below, the Virgin of the Star.

sensibility which gives place to a peculiar form of understanding life the way it is, though in turn, with evident ways of organising and expressing it. Among those events which have an effect on the brotherhoods and their fraternities, are the people of Seville's ways to depict God, to pay homage and to make him present and to take part in the lives of the present-day Sevillians. For this reason, the Rome which is Romanized Seville, that is to say, Sevillianized, are the new impersonal districts, in which the prevailing lifestyle is both neutral and devoid of roots, across the brotherhoods. For this reason Holy Week has an origin and a history, but not an end, it lives on and will continue to live as long as the city.

Virgin of the Brotherhood of San Roque

The Cirineo of San Roque helps to carry the Cross of Jesus. ▶

This can clearly to be seen when Holy Week arrives. The newly formed brotherhoods from the new districts advance from their distant churches, at times marching for more than twelve hours, rather like the legion when it was returning to Rome from some distant province: to the heart of its empire, though never actually having been away from it. When these brotherhoods arrive at the start of the official procession (being the daily route taken by everyone by order of antiquity, which goes from *la Campana* to the Cathedral, through *calle Sierpes,* the *plaza de San Francisco* and the *avenida de la Constitución*) they are greeted by the people occupying the seats and stands and by the authorities or "senados" members of the brotherhoods (in the Campana), civilians (in the plaza de San Francisco) and the religious (in the Cathedral), a kind of baptism takes place in Seville, as if the city bows before the brotherhood acknowledging it to be theirs and in recognition of what they do before the city.

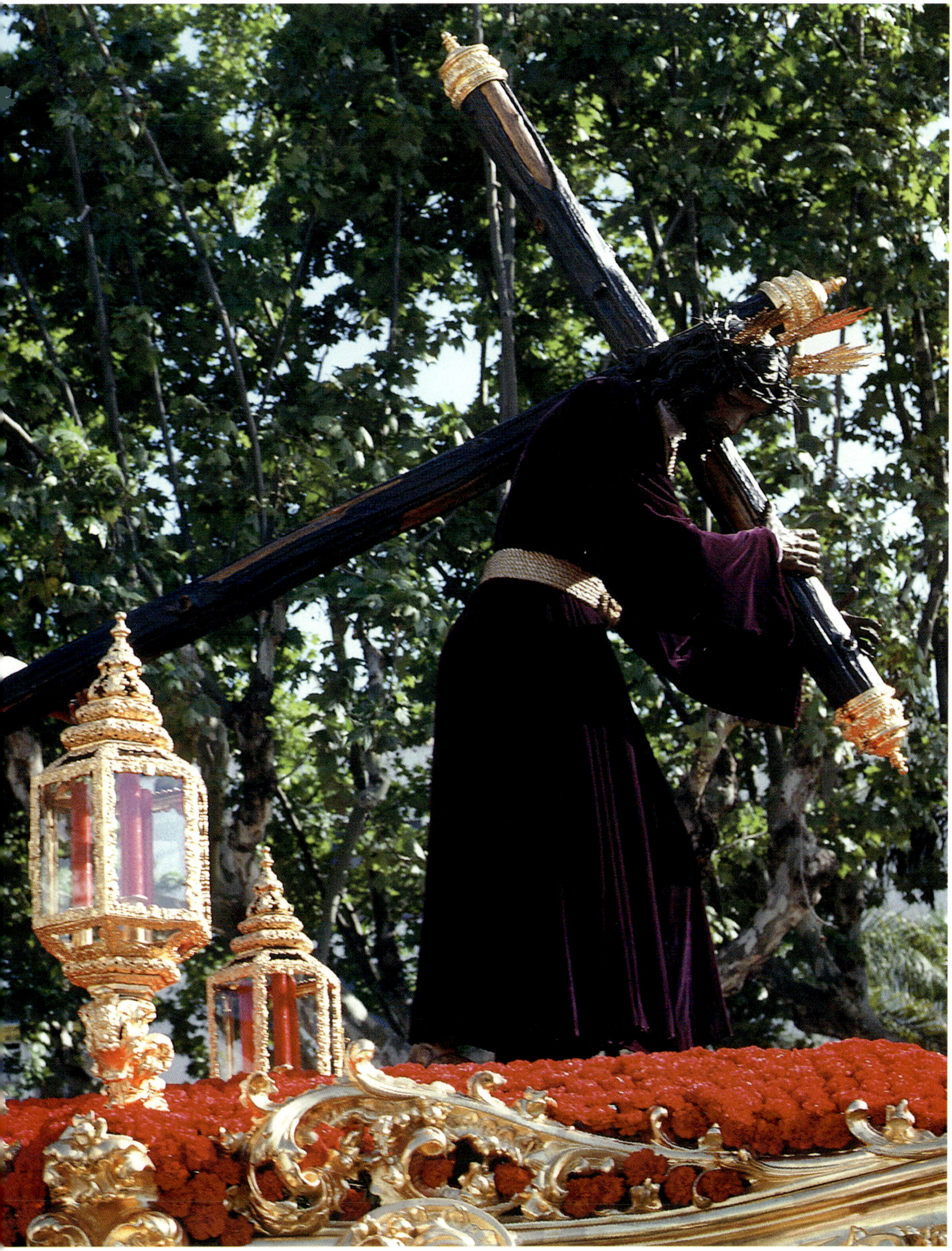

HOLY WEEK

On the following page, paso of Christ of the Brotherhood of Sorrow.

Virgin of Sorrow with Saint John.

Seville's Holy Week is a celebration which is at the same time sacred and profane, religious and civic, ancient and modern, hereditary legacy and present day construction, in which everything is calculated and at the same time spontaneous. Anyone who attends has to take into account that, when the medieval, the baroque, the romantic, the regionalist and the present day are combined, not as a mere accumulation of historical and museum archives, but as a continual reinterpretation and actualisation produced simultaneously by the prevailing and learned classes, by the orthodox and unorthodox, by laymen and clergymen, by believers and disbelievers, by saints and sinners, by creative individuality and collective anonymity, unavoidably it produces the disconcerting but enriching and complex phenomena of which something is equally as certain as it is contrary. There exists not one Holy Week, for which reason there can be no single definition to accurately describe this event. Although yes it is possible to place whoever attends in the most privileged position to be able to see and absorb the event, but above all, what we most anticipate, is to feel a part of the tremendous complexity, vitality, beauty, sensuality, artistic wealth and spiritual profundity. Holy Week is above all, an emotive experience which has a profound effect on the most basic feelings. Love and heartache, life and death, blood and tears, the flesh and the spirit, eternity and finality, the dead and the living, those who fear and those who await, they are all in the street, beneath the bright light of those March and April afternoons, or the mild, clear evenings of Seville's springtime. The event unfolds with gold and silver works, embroidery and velvets, the city's baroque treasures abundant in gold and silver from the Indies. Incense rises in spirals plumes, clambering through the tactile golden air of these Byzantine evenings. Bees fly between the forests of wax and flowers adorning the *pasos*. Heart rending music sounds from the bugles and drums which follow the steps of Christ and the dulcet funeral march following those of the virgins. The eyes of the Nazarenes glisten with emotion beneath the hooded masks. Silent tears fall from the eyes of the devout, whose looks appear to be lost in the flood of memories unleashed by the images they pray for and under whose wing they learnt to pray to. The blood appears to liquefy, and flow, over the sculptured wooden figures which, by candle light, acquire the tepid and absolute authenticity of the flesh: we are in Seville and it is Holy Week. Lets become a part of it.

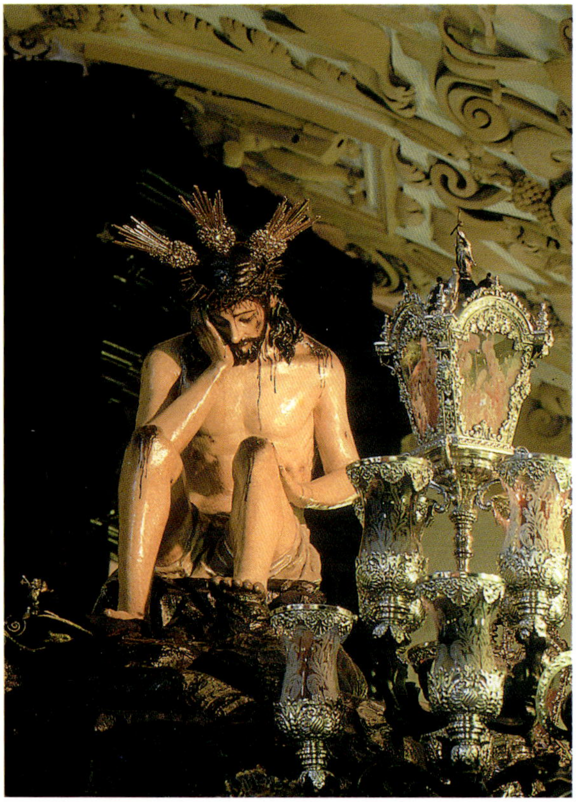
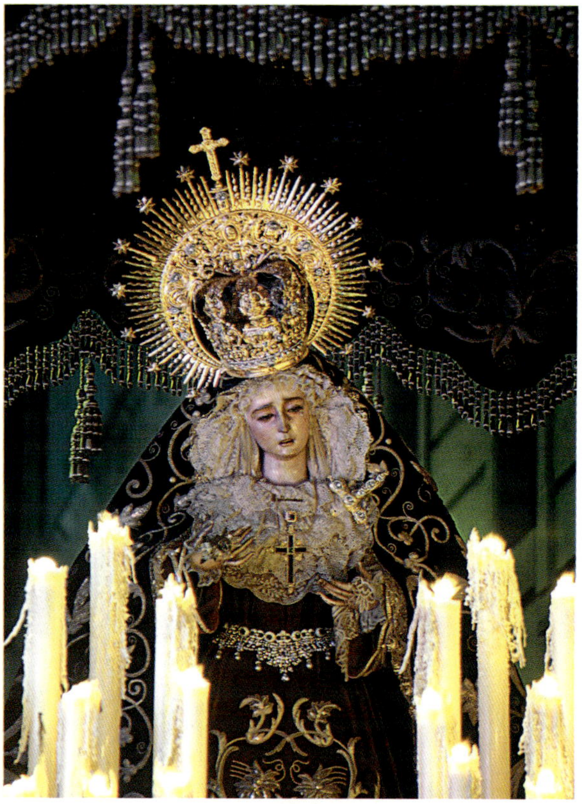
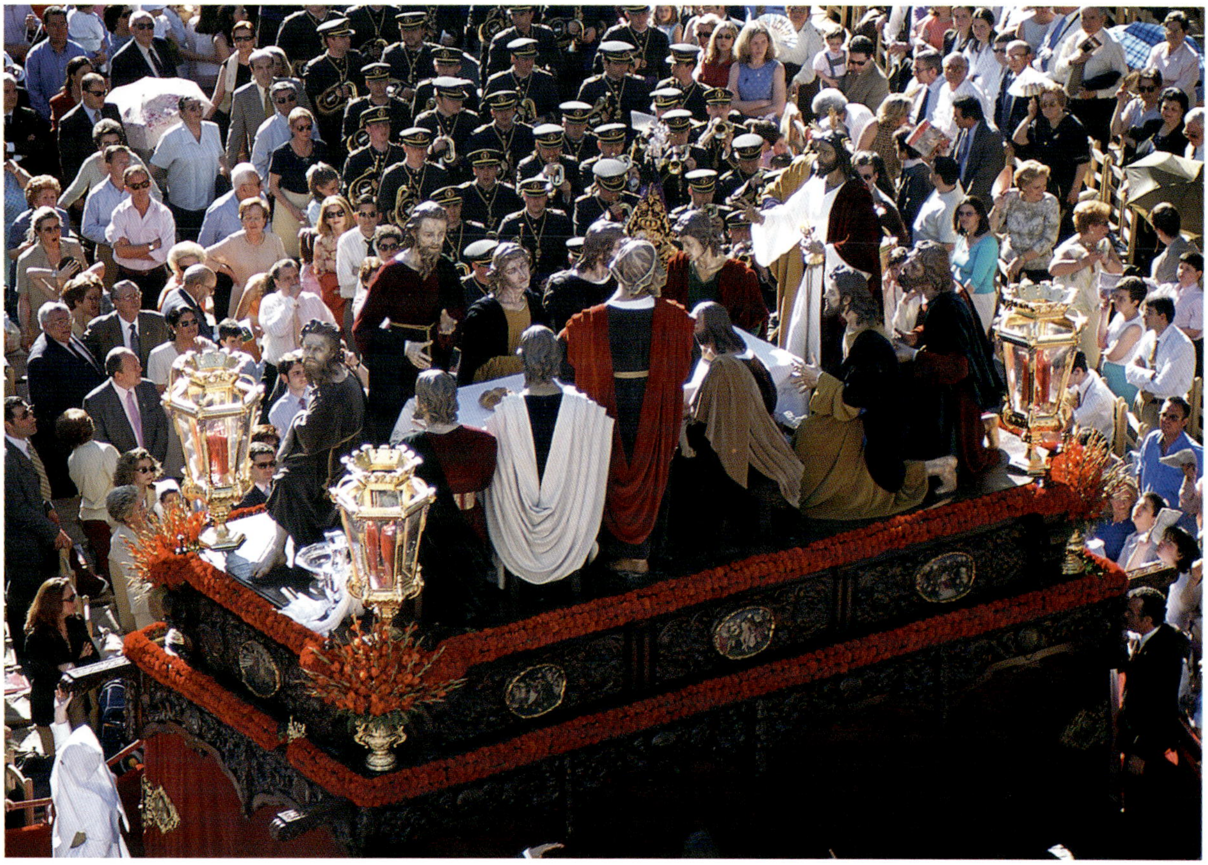

The mystery of Jesus divested.

Canopied paso of the Virgin of the Hiniesta (Broom). ➤

On the former page, different pasos from the Brotherhood of the Supper: above left, Very Holy Christ of Humility and Patience; above right, Our Lady of the Cavern; below, Mystery of the Last Supper.

HOLY WEEK

16

On the following page: The Captive of Holy Genoveva on his paso by the Postigo del Aceite.

Christ of Love.

Holy Week is the universal commemoration, throughout the Catholic Church and the Protestant and Orthodox religions, of the passion, the death and the resurrection of Jesus of Nazareth. It is not celebrated in spring, which at times has been said, being a question of the superimposition of a Christian celebration over other more ancient pagan festivals, who celebrated nature's springtime return to life, but to coincide with the Jewish Passover in which the historic events took place. Although it is not uncommon for Christian celebrations to override pagan festivals, as is the case with Christmas, being the Christian version of the Roman celebration of the birth of the sun, the case of Holy Week is unique. The Passion and the death of Christ are the only dates in his life which are known to be exact, coinciding with the Jewish Passover of Pesaj, which commemorates the liberation of Egypt and which the Jewish faith continues to celebrate on the same date. Jesus had come to Jerusalem to celebrate the Passover and that which for us is the last supper was the ritual meal which initiated it and which was celebrated two thousand years ago as it is today, during the first full moon after the spring equinox. Jesus was detained after this Passover feast, which was celebrated until sunset on the Thursday; was interrogated and tortured in the early hours and on Friday morning, the first day of the Passover; he died on the afternoon of that day, was removed from the cross and buried rapidly before nightfall because the Jews were not permitted to work after sunset on the Friday which inaugurated Saturday, the Hebrew's saints day and the biggest day of the Passover; and resurrected, according to the Christian faith, in the early hours of Sunday morning, his sepulchre having been discovered empty at the start of the day.

Above, Jesus of Pity from the Brotherhood of San Vicente. Left, Christ of Expiration from the Brotherhood of the Museum.

The Church has faithfully commemorated these crucial events, the *Pascua de Resurrección* (Easter) being the foundation, for this reason it is known to be the "Celebration of celebrations" and the "Solemnity of solemnities" – respecting the dates in which the Jewish Passover took place. In the year 325, at the *Concilio de Nicea*, (council), all the churches agreed to celebrate the Easter resurrection, and for this reason Holy Week, guided by the Jewish Passover, that is to say, the Sunday following the first full moon after the spring equinox. The changes made to the western calendar in 1582, beneath the papacy of Gregory XIII, introduced a gap of some days which separated the Catholic Holy Week from the Jewish Passover. Protestants were guided by the Gregorian calendar, but the Orthodox continued to celebrate the exact historic date. Despite this slight discrepancy in days between Catholics and Protestants, on the one side, and

Virgin of the Waters from the Brotherhood of the Museum.

Orthodox on the other, Holy Week is a universal Christian celebration. Nevertheless, the Church has recognized that the liturgical celebration, whilst safeguarding the fundamentals, has to correspond with the cultures from different nations. Out of this diversity towards the identical and this unity within the diverse, very different liturgical approaches have developed to commemorate the sacred mysteries of the Passion, the death and the resurrection of Christ. Amongst them, that which Seville has been creating since Middle Ages, after the city was re-conquered by Fernando III in the year 1248, founding, only a century later, the most ancient brotherhood still in existence today.

Virgin of the Sweet Name. ➤

Left, exit of the palio (canopied float) from San Esteban. Below, Christ of the Good Death from the Brotherhood of the Students.

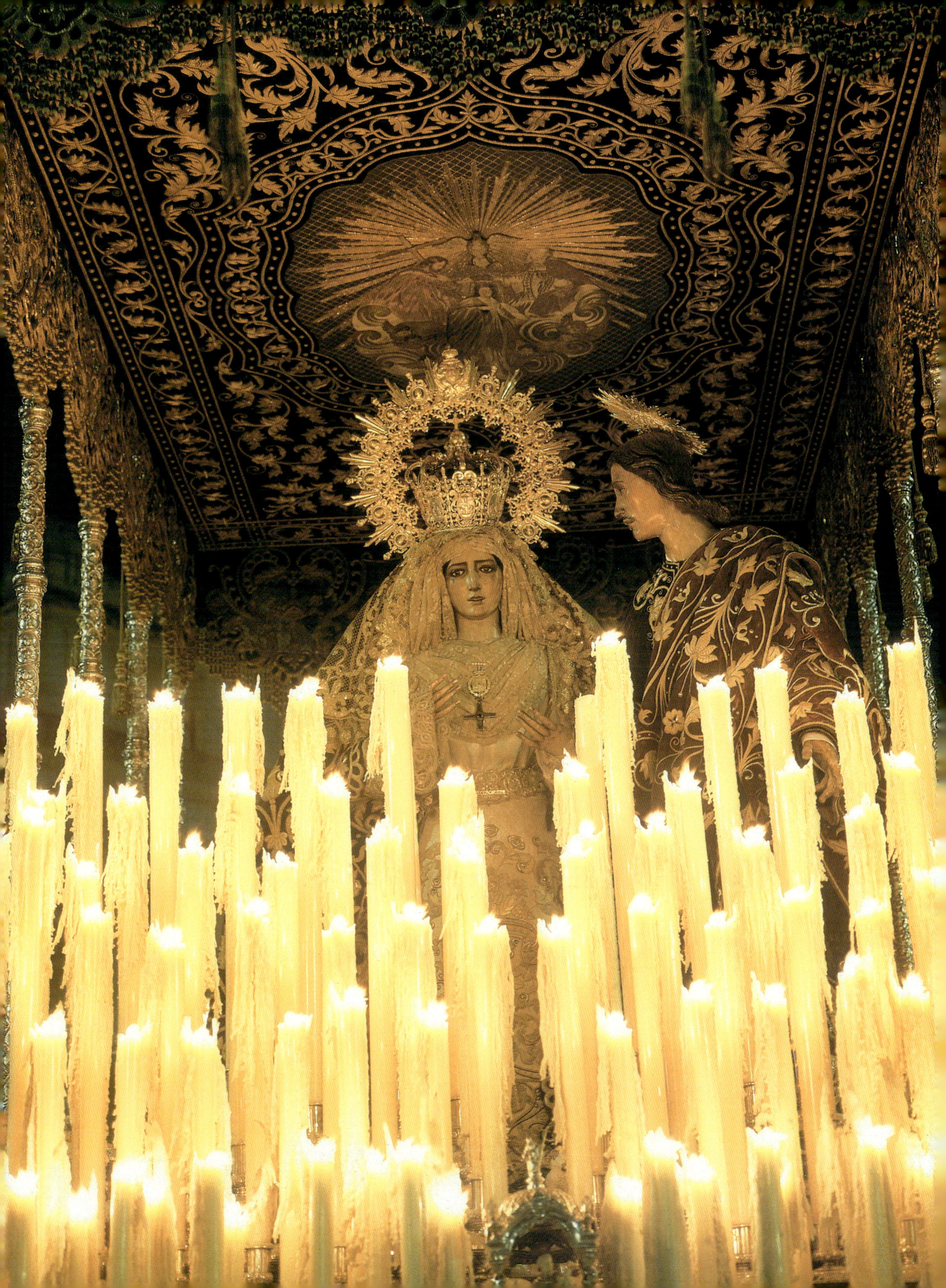

HOLY WEEK IN SEVILLE

22

Christ of Salvation from the Brotherhood of San Bernardo.

The second mainstay of Seville's Holy Week, after what is deemed to be the appropriate and universal liturgical celebration adapted to the character and culture of the city, is their homage to the sacred images. Also in this respect the most remote origin of Holy Week is from Nicea. If the first Council of the fore mentioned Nicea, in the 4th Century, fixed the date of the celebration universally, three centuries later, in the year 787, the second Council of Nicea reinforced the importance of the images as opposed to the iconoclasts, taking naturalization papers in the Christian homage to the representations of Jesus Christ, the Virgin and the saints. The Incarnation, represented as human flesh, of God in Jesus of Nazareth, permits the representation of images which reproduce the body and the face of Christ to be as the artists visualize them in the light of the threefold Gospel, the Churches teaching and its special mastery and artistic inspiration.
As usually happens with liturgy, each period and each culture has represented Christ by their own artistic means: the Good Shepherd by the first Roman Christians, the severe Romanesque crucifix, the triumphant stylish crucifixes of the gothic Christ Pantocrator or the suffering and realistic baroque

HOLY WEEK IN SEVILLE

*Right, Virgin of the Rule from the Brotherhood of the Bakers.
Below, Mystery of the Seven Words.*

crucifixes. Seville has chosen baroque artistry as that which best corresponds to the city's sensibility, preserving to the faith above all those images from the 17th and 18th Centuries, carving in the baroque style, additions to these historical relics up until the present time and casting aside throughout history, the former gothic images. In fact, there remains in the procession now only one Gothic Christ, that of the Vera Cruz, and one from the 16th century, that of the Expiración del Museo. But we leave the topic here. Now that we have outlined the universal origins of the liturgical commemoration and its homage to the images which are central to all the Holy Week celebrations, the moment has come to trace a brief history of that of Seville.

The conformation process of the Sevillian fiesta is inseparable from the city's political, economic, social and artistic history and its mentalities, in an extensive chronological arc which runs from the end of the Middle Ages (in as much as the most ancient

Left, Virgin of the Palm from the Brotherhood of the Good End. Right, Christ of Burgos.

The Piety of the Baratillo, from the Barrio del Arenal district. ▶

brotherhood, the Silent was founded in 1340) until the present day (the last brotherhood to be incorporated in Holy Week, that of *Cerro,* was in 1989, with more awaiting the ecclesiastical authority to do so) across the four decisive Stations of the Cross brought together in moments of the city's transformation: the Seville which runs from the end of the Middle Ages to the Age of Discovery (14th and 15th centuries), the baroque (17th century) the Late Romanticism (19th century) and Regionalism (at the beginning of the 20th century).

The origins have to lie in the medieval atonements, which in Seville were symbolised by the public penitence by the devout founders of the brotherhood of *Silencio* (the Silent), known for this reason as the *Madre* and *Maestra* (mother and master) of the Brotherhoods of Seville who, preceded by a crucifix, went in the early hours of Good Friday from the Omnium Santorum church in calle Feria to the San Lázaro hospital, located outside the city's walls. To closer resemble their divine image, these men went dressed in tunics of course cloth, their heads covered by wigs encircled by crowns of thorns and carrying crosses, for which reason since that time on, those accompanying the sacred images on the brotherhoods entourage are called Nazarenes in respect to their identification with Jesus of Nazareth. Of the medieval Holy Week there remains practically nothing more in the present day version than this Silent brotherhood, the Christ of the Vera Cruz and the link with the recollection of the Passion to the pious practice of the *Vía Crucis,* in which the Stations of the Cross have brought inspiration to the images and intriguing groups of images representing scenes and carried upon the *pasos or* floats.

HOLY WEEK IN SEVILLE

25

Jesus of the Passion.

In the 16th century the Duke of Tarifa returned from a pilgrimage to the Holy Land, when they measured the distance from the Roman *pretorio* where Pontius Pilate condemned Christ, and from where he departed carrying the cross, to mount Calvary. Taking as a point of departure his own palace in the San Esteban district, known since this time as the *Casa de Pilatos* and continuing along the line of the Roman aqueduct known as the *Caños de Carmona,* next to which ran one of the routes of entry into Seville, he reproduced the distance and there where it corresponded to Calvary, he constructed a shrine which harboured a cross, still in existence today and known as the *Cruz del Campo.* Many pious associations take the *Vía Crucis* between *Casa de Pilatos* and the *Cruz del Campo,* reproducing in this way the actual route taken by the Lord with the cross on his back.

Nazarenes from the Brotherhood of Montesión. ➤

Mystery of the Exaltation, known as "Los Caballos" (The Horses).

*Above: left, Nazarenes from the Brotherhood of the Negritos; Right, Christ of the Foundation.
Below, Nazarenes from the Brotherhood of the Fifth Anxiety.*

The Deposition of Christ from the Brotherhood of the Fifth Anxiety.

Departure of the Passion. ➤

Virgin of Victory from the Brotherhood of the Cigar Makers.

It was in the 16th and 17th centuries, in conjunction with Seville's American heyday, when Semana Santa became defined in respect to the entourages, itineraries, design of the *pasos* (above all those of Christ, since they were to be profoundly transformed in the second half of the 19th century and the first thirty years of the 20th century) and the iconography of the sacred images. Among the entourage were masked penitents carrying candles (the brothers of light) and those beating themselves with whips (the brothers of blood which disappeared at the beginning of the 19th century). Until 1640 each brotherhood followed its own itinerary which barely left the limits of the district or community in which it lived, but since this date it was made an obligation for all the brotherhoods to make their place of penance the Cathedral, except for those of Triana, who were not able to cross the river by means of the bridge of boats which at the time connected the district to Seville, and made their penance in the parish of Santa Ana, until the construction of the Triana bridge in 1830 enabled them to go to the Cathedral. After the 1640 arrangement, the progressive coincidence of all the brotherhoods making their way to the same point, the Cathedral, obliged them to define timetables and itineraries to avoid conflicts, at the time which little by little, came to define an identical route for all which eventually came to be recognised as the official route, which was to reach its peak in the civic and bourgeois Holy Week of the second half

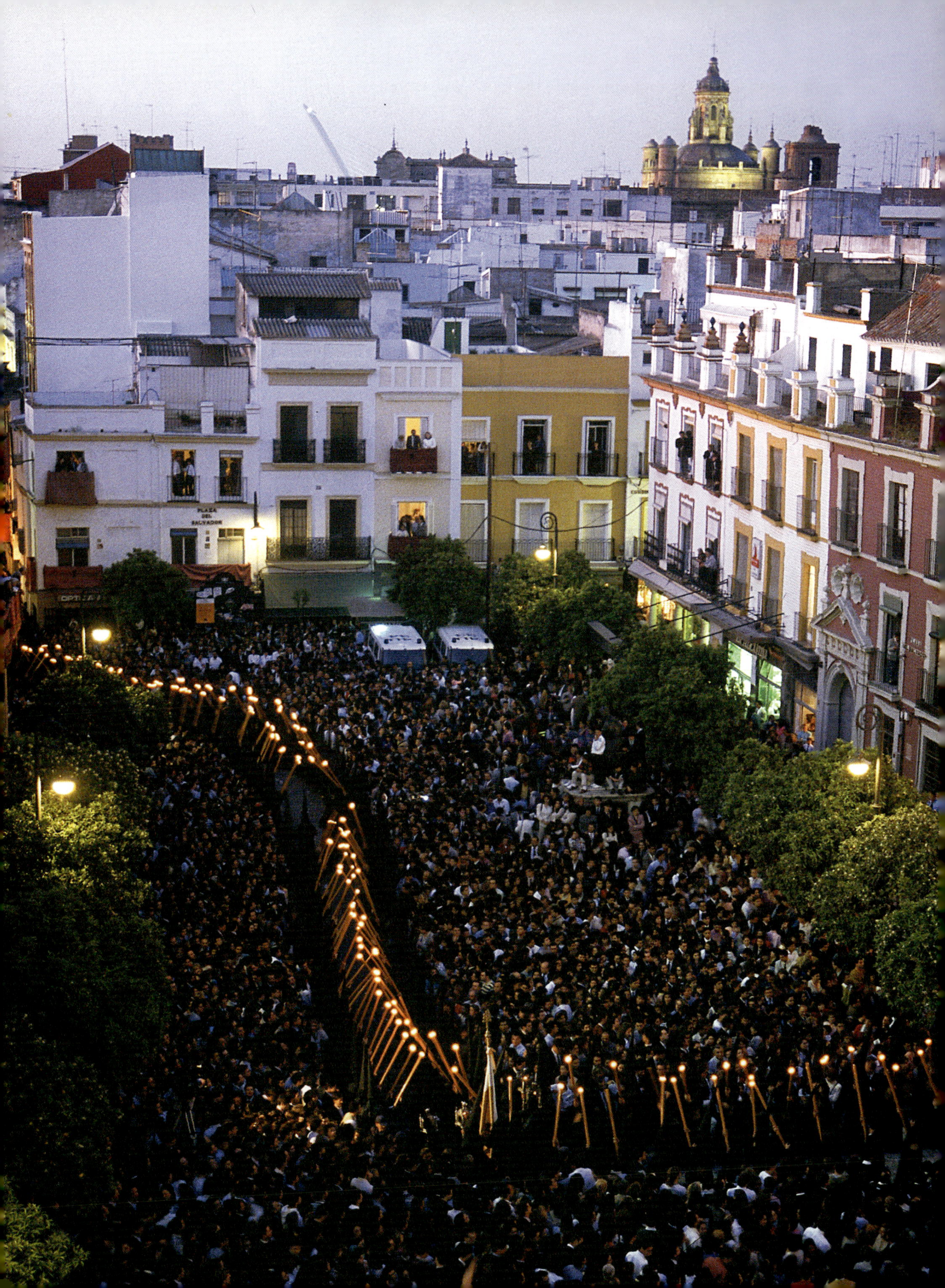
PLAZA DEL SALVADOR

of the 19th century and continues to the present day, beginning at La Campana and finishing at the Cathedral, along calle Sierpes, through the plaza de San Francisco and the avenida de la Constitución.

The floats upon which the images are carried were also found in the 17th century, their definitive creation around the canonical model transformed into the splendid *paso* representing God the *Gran Poder,* still in being, with slight modifications, the same as that which was in the dawn procession sculptured by the great religious sculpture Gijón, the creator of the *Christo del Cachorro,* at the end of the same century. Few of the floats have been preserved from this century due to the logical deterioration provoked by their use which includes, in addition to their annual *armá* (mounting) and *desarmá* (dismounting), exposure to inclement changes in the spring weather which at times castigated the brotherhoods with torrential downpours, and from being subjected to trends and disrespect towards the decorative and applied artworks which became less respected over the years. In addition to the *Gran Poder,* other surviving floats from the 17th century are those of *Amor,* (Love), *Jesús Nazareno* or *la Mortaja* (the shroud).

In terms of the most important, the Sevillian iconographical portrayal of the sacred images, remains firmly established, up until the present time as in the 17th century by sculptors such as Andres de Ocampo (Christ of the Foundation), Francisco de Ocampo (Jesús of Nazareth of Silence, Christ of Calvary), Martinez Montañés (Jesus of the Passion), Juan de Mesa (Jesus of the Gran Poder and the Crucifix of Love, the Conversion y Buena Muerte), Pedro Roldán (Lord of Silence before Herod's scorn, Nazarene of the O, Christ and mystery figures of the Fifth Anxiety) and Francisco Antonio Gijón (Christ of the Cachorro). It could be said that the great Sevillian school of thought was initiated at the beginning of the 17th century with the Christ of the Chalices (which was not in the procession but could be seen in the Cathedral) and Jesus of Passion both by Martinez Montañés, and finished with the prodigious Christ of the Expiration – known as el Cachorro – which Gijón sculptured at the end of this same century. Curiously, the creators behind the most celebrated and devout virgins – have not been able to be documented, although they are known to be from the 17th century.

HOLY WEEK IN SEVILLE

On the former page, Brotherhood of the Valley.
Above: Crown of thorns.
Below, altar boy from the palio (canopied float).

Virgin of the Valley. ▶

The Lord with the Cross on his Shoulder, from the Brotherhood of the Valley.

HOLY WEEK IN SEVILLE

34

*"Jesús del Gran Poder".
La Madrugada (The early hours
of the morning).* ➤

*Our Lord Jesus of Nazareth
from the Brotherhood of Silence.*

*Palio of the Virgin of Conception
from the Brotherhood of Silence.*

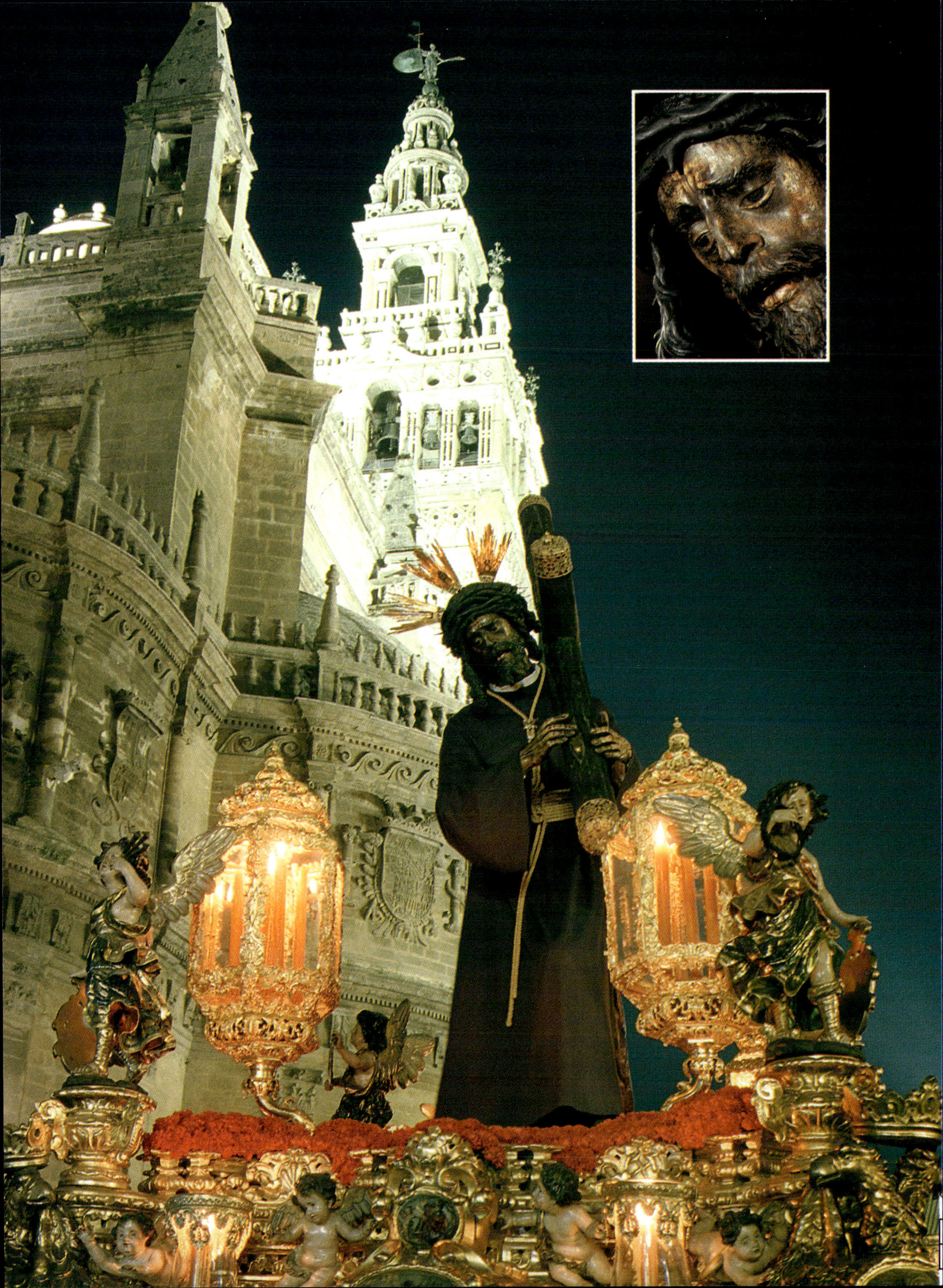

*Above: left, Nazarenes of the Macarena;
Right, Our Lord Jesus of Judgement.
Left, the band of bugles and drums from
the Centuria Macarena.*

Overshadowing the great baroque representation of Holy Week during Seville's times of splendour, the celebration followed the decline of the city. The 18th century and the initial years of the 19th century were particularly tragic times for both: the population was decimated by the plague and reduced to half and its commercial monopoly with the Indies, which had been the source of its wealth and splendour, was transferred to Cadiz. The French invasion was the final straw resulting fatal for a city already decimated and impoverished and for the brotherhoods, many of which were pillaged by the invaders. The subsequent alienation by Mendizabal (1834), with the desecration of

First design of the Virgin of Hope Macarena.

La Macarena and La Centuria at "armaos" close to the entrance of the Basilica Friday at midday.

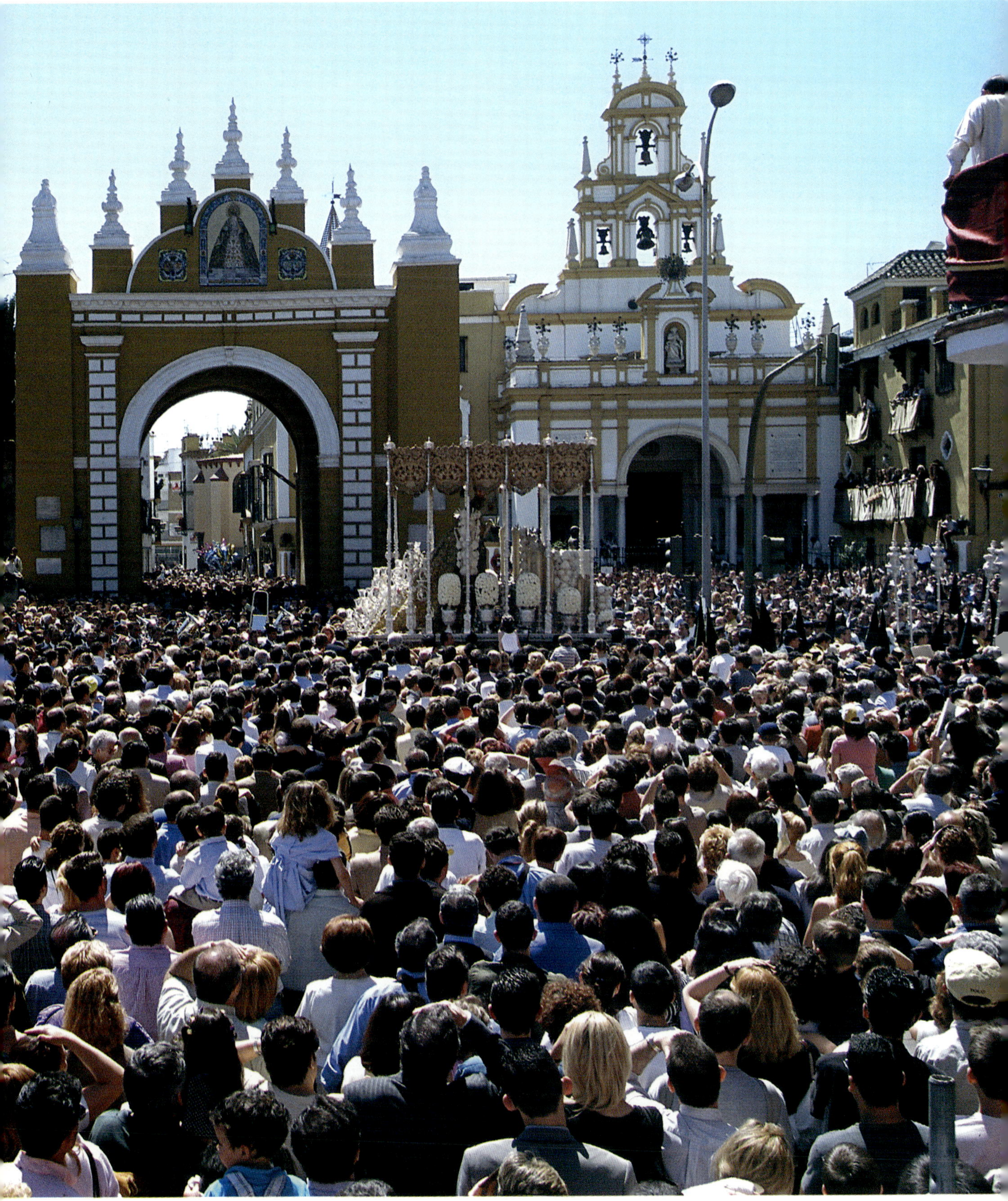

HOLY WEEK IN SEVILLE

Left, Holy Christ of Calvary.

churches and convents and many the brotherhoods were expelled, though they had lived here for centuries. One of the city's historians almost gave most of the corporations up as lost until 1840. Nevertheless, the city was to be reborn only a few years later at the hands of the rising bourgeois aristocracy, gathered around the *"corte chica"*, the court established by the dukes of Montpensier after becoming resident in the San Telmo palace, which brought the declined celebration back to life. This authentic rebirth of Holy Week included all the essential elements inherited from the baroque but with a less dramatic, more pleasant feeling to it, more festive and less penitential, more civic than ecclesiastical, a time when they formally redefined above all the ornamental and the musical elements: in the second half of this century the new canopy floats were born enriched by another new concept, that of embroidery, the culmination of which was to be represented by the gifted embroiderers, the Antúnez brothers and for which equally new funeral marches were composed for band music, a legacy from the Romantic funeral march, a

Palio of the Virgin of the Presentation, from the Brotherhood of Calvary.

HOLY WEEK IN SEVILLE

42

Our Lord Jesus of Salvation, known as "Er Manué". ➤

Virgin of Anxiety and Nazarenes from the Brotherhood of the Gypsies.

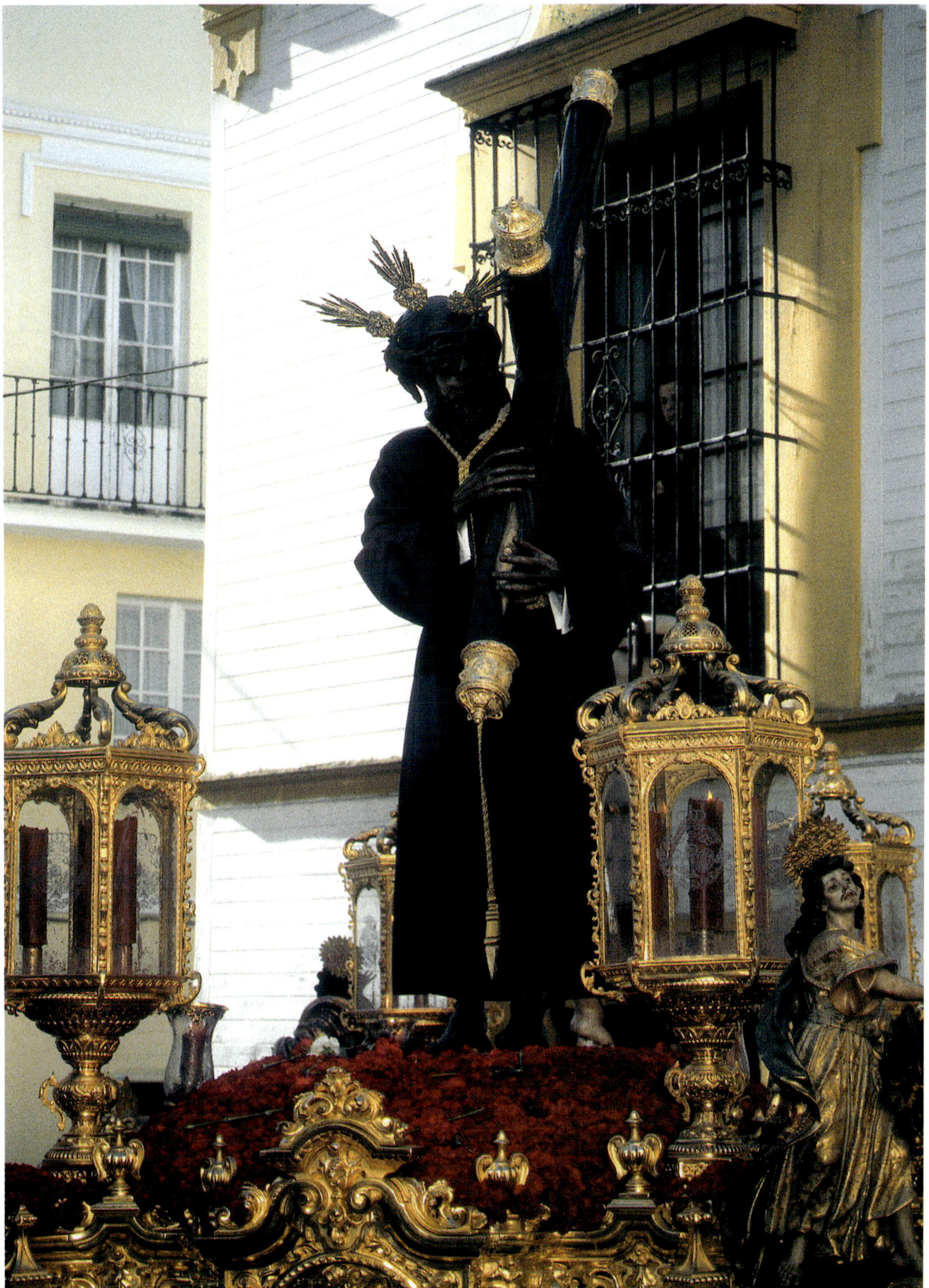

HOLY WEEK IN SEVILLE

Christ of the Three Fallen, from the Brotherhood La Esperanza de Triana.

time when the crucifix's were followed by the marching sounds of bugles and drums as testimony to the military presence and to both the Crucifix's and the Virgins and to whom they sang *saetas* (flamenco-style songs sung on religious occasions), as an expression of the new general feeling. It is significant that this "new" Holy Week united with the then recently created Feria de Abril in its new representation (in respect to the agricultural, industrial and tourist promotion of the city) of the original "spring festival", being announced as such in the posters specifically made to publicise Seville's festivals.

In the first thirty years of the 20th century, in the context of a city reborn, as if it had returned to the golden ages of the 16th and 17th centuries, that is before the prospect of the 1929 Exhibition, and it was reinvented with words by the writers of "Sevillian Idealism" (José Maria Izquierdo, Manuel Chaves Nogales, Rafael Laffón, Joaquín Romero Murube, Juan Sierra) and with new urbanisations and buildings by regional architects (Aníbal González, Talavera, Espiau, Goméz Millán), the Holy Week recognised as the biggest and the most recent transformation in its history up to the present time with the regional and the customary being combined with the baroque and the antiquated. In the same way that a great number of Seville's present day "traditional" features were created in the first thirty years of the 20th century, the Santa Cruz district, plaza de España, avenida de la Constitución, the María Luísa park, it could be said that the present day Holy Week is that which was created in these same years. Not by way of a

The Esperanza de Triana returning to their chapel. ➤

Our Lady of the Esperanza de Triana.

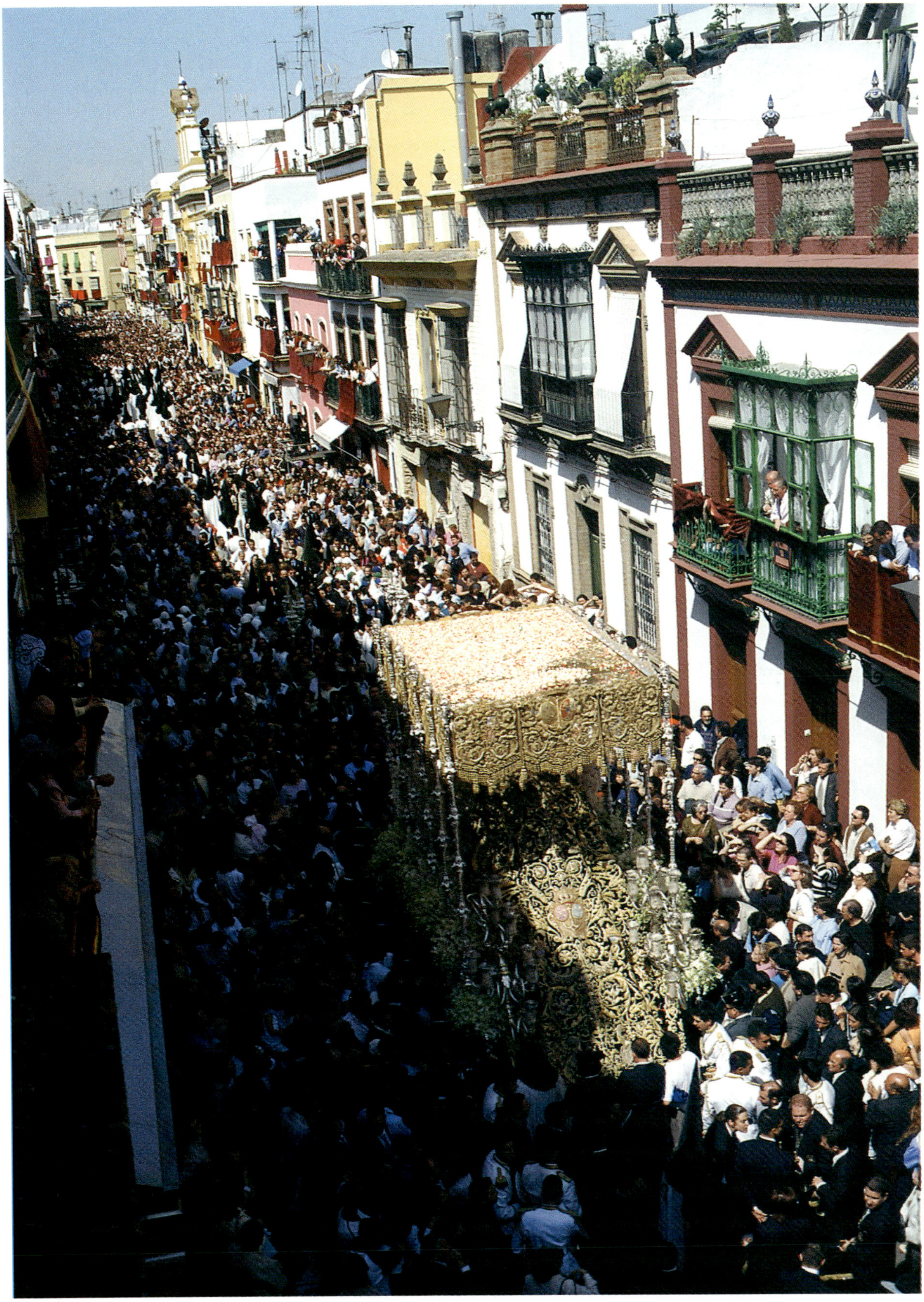

The Solitude of San Buenaventura.

On the following double page the Brotherhood of the O, on the way to Triana bridge.

substitution, but a reinvention and integration of the new with the old which was at the same time an inspiration. The same as has happened in the plaza de la Virgin de los Reyes, the monumental heart of Seville, where the Almohade Giralda (cathedral tower), the gothic cathedral, the renaissance Royal Chapel, and the baroque archiepiscopal palace blend with the new city planning represented by the central fountain and the beautiful buildings at the start of calle Mateos Gago, all of which were constructed in the twenties, likewise with Holy week there remains some of the ancient elements and practices, above all the images and floats of Christ, but integrated with a new world.

The Holy Week experienced a formal revolution in these years which could be symbolised by the embroiderer Juan Manuel Rodriguez Ojeda, who redefined a great part of the formal aspect of the festival just in the arch comprised of two revolutionary cloaks which were designed for the Esperanza Macarena: one in mesh (1900) and one in lamé (1930). In the thirties the sweetly severe "romantic" canopied float or *palios* acquired a new and unusual grace, abandoning their uniform structure, the embroidered leaves and the dark velvets, thanks, above all to the aforementioned Rodríguez Ojeda, who introduced coloured velvets, embroidered with transparent mesh and coloured silk threads, and broke with the straight structure of the of fall of the canopies to make them more jagged. A new hooded gown was designed for the Macarena brotherhood, which the other fraternities were to copy, as well as the Roman centurion robes for the famous "armaos".

Brotherhood of the Wheelwrights.

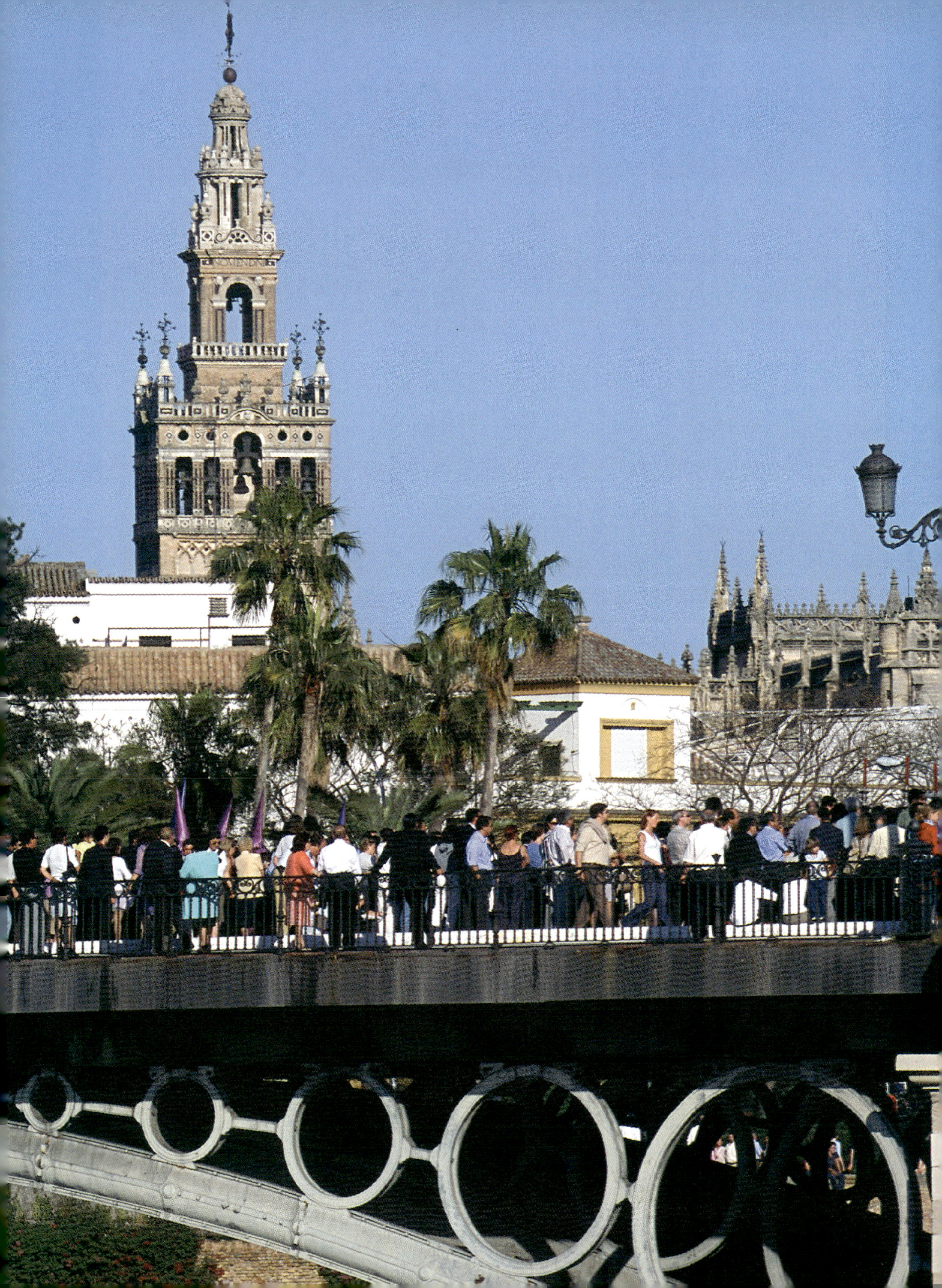

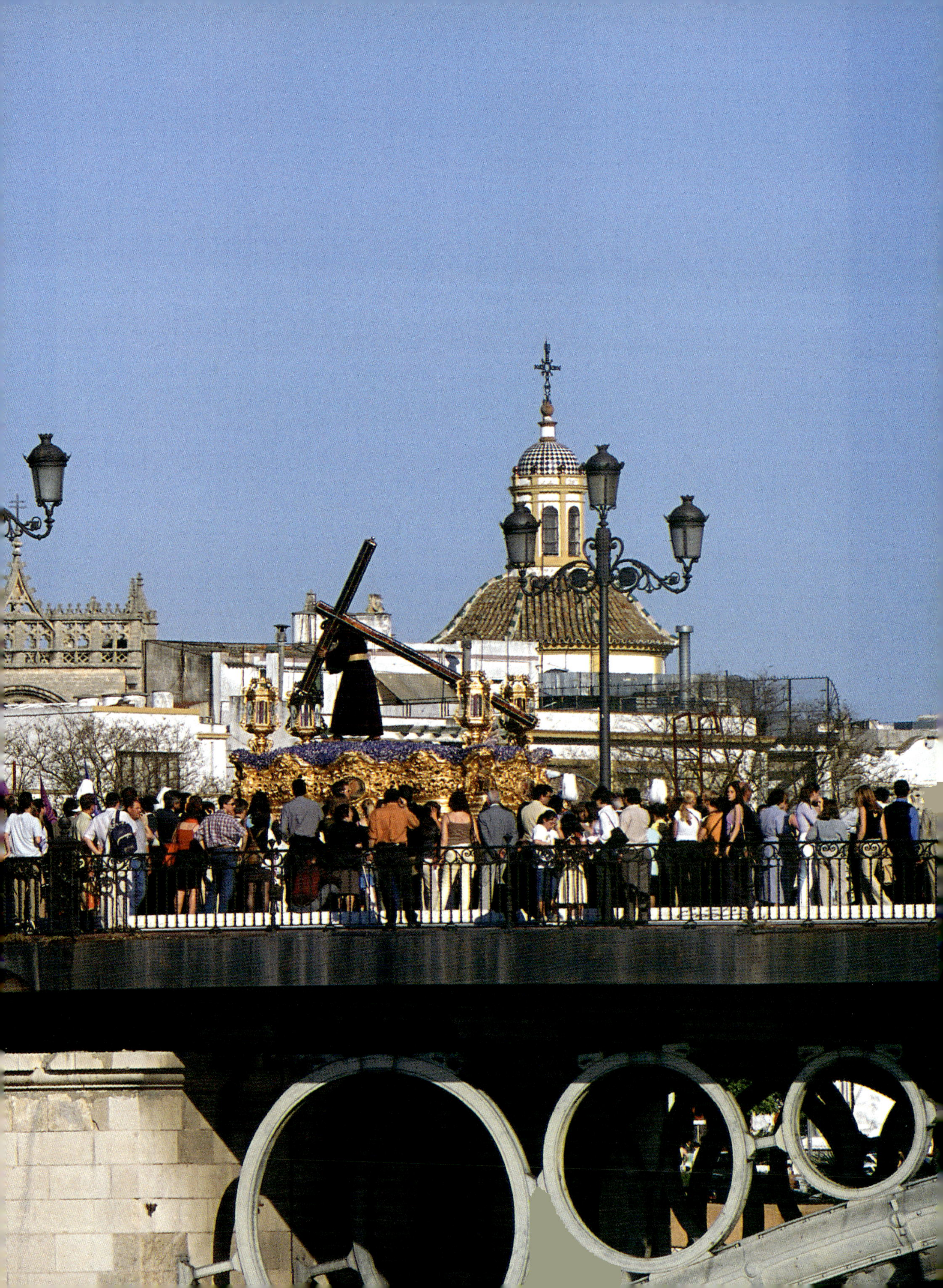

HOLY WEEK IN SEVILLE

and drum section within the traditional structure of the band, creating a new kind of processional march which was surprisingly joyful and graceful, such as the extremely popular "Estrella Sublime" or the "Pasan los campanilleros", the perfect expression of the colourful joy of this local and traditional Holy Week. These compositions by Font and Farfán, together with the most ancient and romantic "Virgen del Valle" by Gómez Zarzuela, from 1899, have become up until the present time, the most popular in Seville and among the canonical processional compositions, up to the point where "Amargura" is considered to be the Holy Week hymn.

Nazarenos de La O before the door of their temple.

Virgen de La O.

Rodríguez Ojeda has been involved with almost all of the outstanding canopied floats in Seville, Macarena, Mayor Dolor and Traspaso, Amargura, Valle, Victoria, Presentación, which give some idea of the importance of his transformational work. Together with him, the craftsmen from Olmo, with their splendid embroidered works of the Concepción, the Patrocinio and las Lagrimas, represent the most highly respected embroidery from 20th century Seville.
In parallel, composers loyal to musical nationalism such as Font created in the tens and twenties new funeral marches such as "Amargura" and "Soleá dame la mano", and the military musician Farfán, incorporating a bugle

HOLY WEEK IN SEVILLE

Costaleros (Float or Paso bearers).

All the Holy Week music is nowadays reinvented, the only remaining piece from old being the *saetillas* which are performed by a trio made up of a bassoon, clarinet and oboe in the dazzling at the same time as it is severe Jesus of Nazareth entourage. Similar *saetillas* nowadays accompany the brotherhoods in their funereal opulence in this Holy Week scene, such as those of San Vicente, Santa Cruz, Santa Marta, or the Mortaja. The heart rending sounds of the bugles and drums with their martial and manly tones accompany the steps of Christ. Dulcet melancholic tones or delicately graceful band marches accompany the floats. And the silence, as an expression of the greatest impact, envelops the most imposing and severe of the images, such as Amor (Love), Buena Muerte (Good Death), Pasión (Passion), Gran Poder (God), Calvario (Calvary) or Tres Caídos (theThree Fallen) and San Isidoro.

It is by no coincidence that these years, 1900 to 1930, when the art of bearing the floats came to be appreciated and defined, were also the golden age of the *saetas*. The dock loaders who carried the floats, or *costaleros*, derived from the word "costal" relating to the bundle worn to save them from being injured by the chaffing with the wood which supported the neck to bear the float, blinded by the velvet skirting which was to hide them, obeying the orders of their foreman or *capataces,* being the same who commanded the workers loading and unloading the boats in Seville's port. Some of these foremen can be seen in front of the floats, giving orders with their popular characteristic gestures, they soon became famous for the mastery and grace with which they carried this out. So, little by little, the need to be burdened with the floats or *pasos* in order to carry them to the Cathedral was transformed into an art by

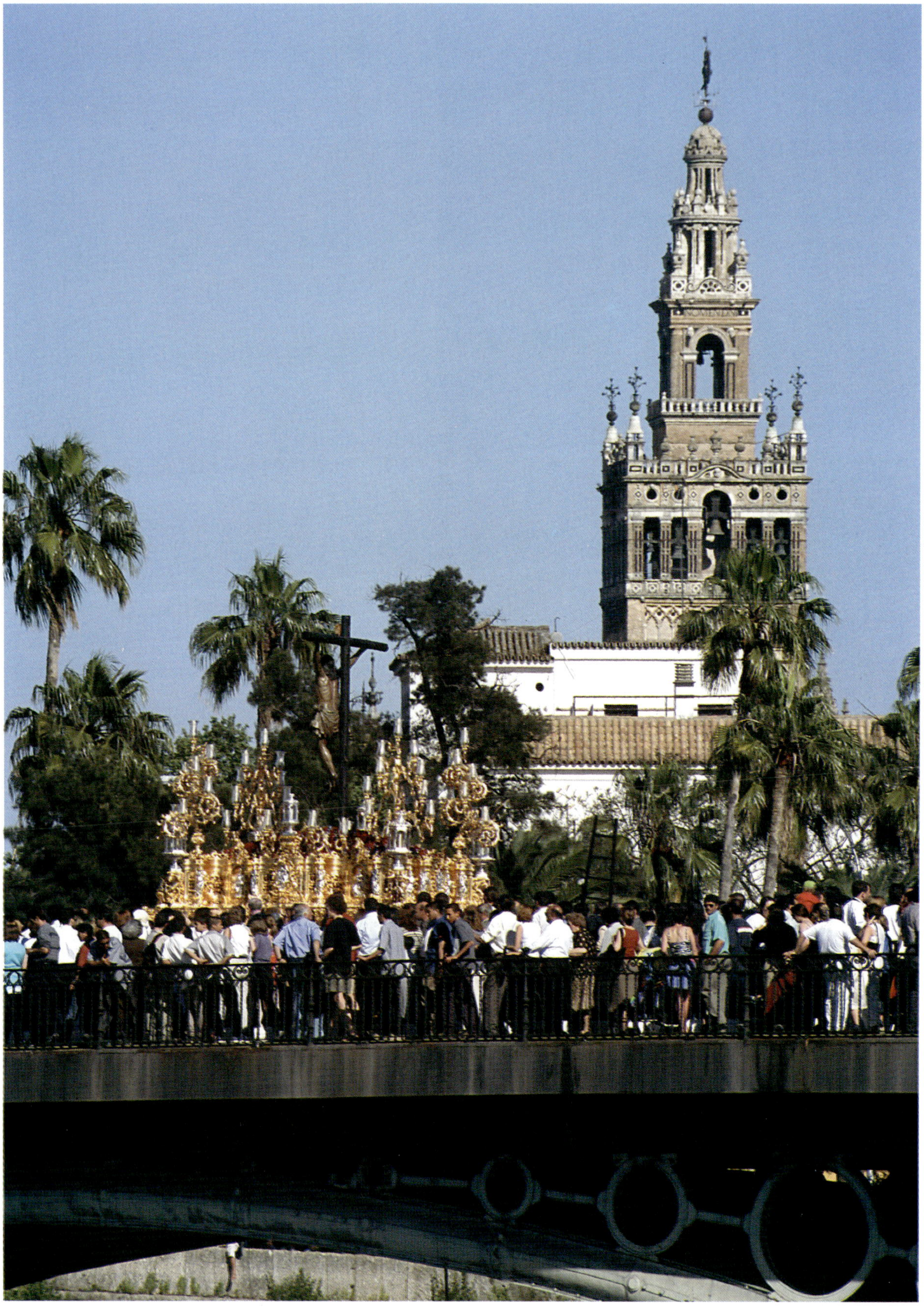

Brotherhood of the Cachorro: above the Virgin of Patronage; and on the former page the Christ of the Expiration, known as "El Cachorro".

the *capataces* and *costaleros* to convey the *palios*, the elaborate canopied floats gracefully and those of Christ dramatically. The popularity of the flamenco song at the end of the 19th century and above all in the beginning of the 20th century, had the effect that, legendary flamenco singers such as Torres, Centeno, la Niña de los Peines or la Niña de la Alfalfa established the *saeta* as a major art. Legend brings together the art of the *capataces* and *costaleros* with that of the *saeteros*, relating that the custom of swinging the *palios* came about when Centeno sang such a splendid *saeta* to the Macarena brotherhood, in the calle Sierpes that the *costaleros*, wishing to hear it in its entirety, advanced so slowly once the *paso* was hoisted that they appeared to be walking without moving from the spot. The *saetas* expressed a new commonly shared feeling over the pain and injustice suffered by the people and the carpenter's son unjustly condemned by political and religious power. In the impressive "Salmo de

Mystery of the Sacred Shroud.

Jesús del Gran Poder", written in the thirties, the Sevillian journalist Nuñez Herrara called to the Lord "Honourable father and most excellent worker", who shared in "the proletarians suffering" and saw in his tunic "wood shavings from the carpenter Joseph".

Holy Week has not ceased to evolve since the thirties, it is above all, a living celebration, but always within the parameters of the model established in the first thirty years of the twentieth century. That being the classic canon invoked when some aesthetic transgression comes into play together with the ambience born from the new ceremonial and musical worlds.

All this historical legacy, art and tradition remain alive and well thanks to the power of the images. If the traveller wants to know the truth behind Seville's Holy Week, he has know the importance of the images in the lives of the people of Seville, up to the point where they are integrated with and become a part of their daily lives, saying their prayers to them or simply gazing longingly and lovingly at them. For this, it is sufficient only to enter the bars and see their photographs taking pride of place, to visit the great department stores and see them stuck to the cash registers; to see the people sat in empty churches, outside the hours of worship, contemplating them engrossed; stand in the doorway of Montesión, of la Estrella, of la Macarena, of the Gran Poder or of la Esperanza de Triana and see how those who come to say their daily prayers enter, equally with the respect demanded by the house of God and the confidence to do so in a fitting manner, to visit "their" Christ or "their" Virgin, named as such with a possessive, not to denote exclusion nor much less pagan misunderstanding, but this intimate form of love based on total surrender and absolute possession which in traditional cultures only applies to blood relations. It is "their" Christ or "their" Virgin because, at the same time, the devout also belong to them with this unique form of mutual understanding within paternity, maternity and the relationship; the possessive having the same significance as that used by the mothers in Seville's *barrios* or districts, when they refer to their sons, saying "my Antonio", "my Rocío", or "my Paco". Up to the point where the people of Seville, contravening theology, have always called God the *Gran Poder* "my father", ("pare mío", in the ancient *saetas*), for which reason, when their church was named Basílica Menor (the lesser Basilica), the brotherhood requested that it be

Our Lady of Monserrat. ➤

Conversion of the Good Thief from the Brotherhood of Monserrat.

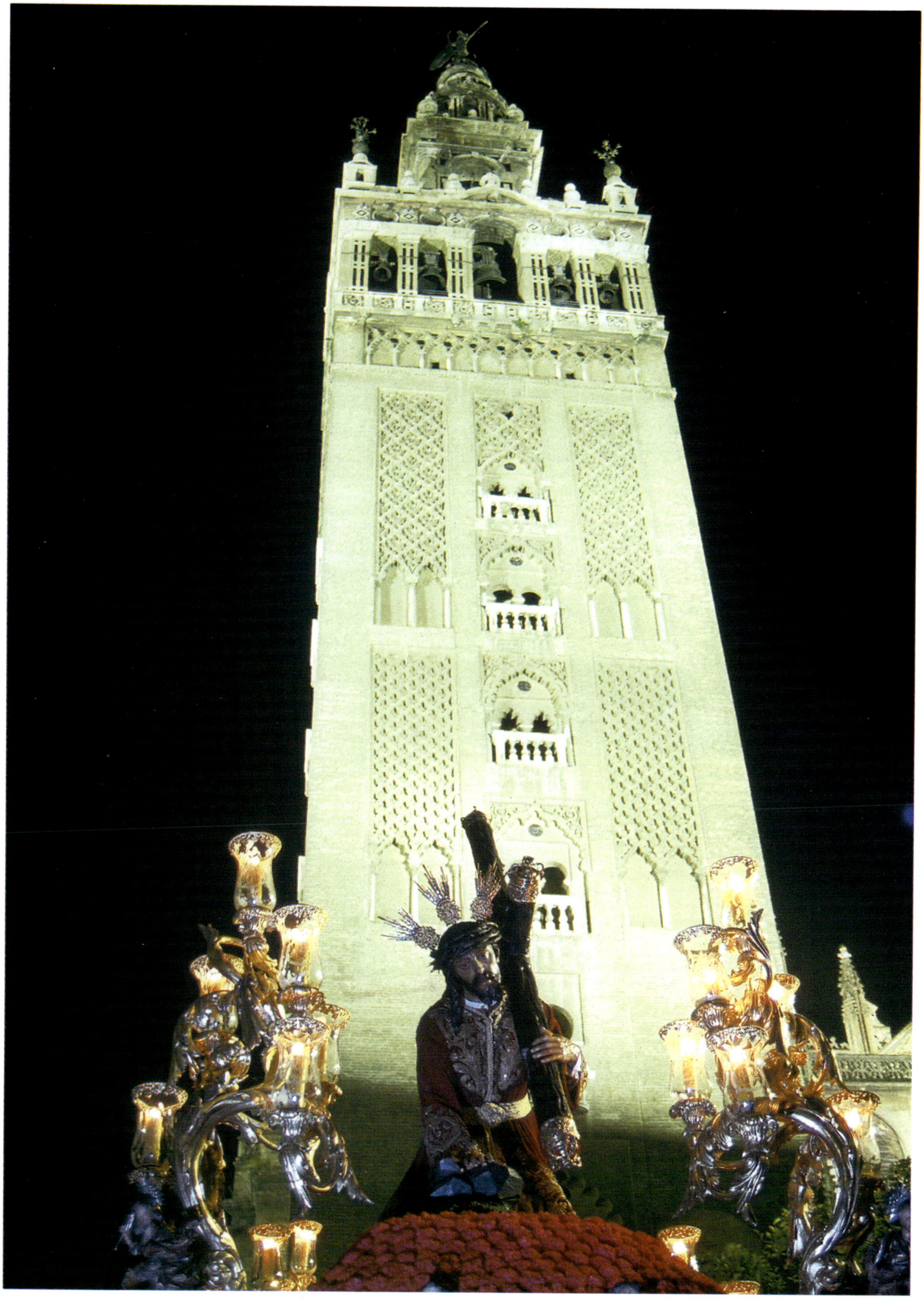

Brotherhood of the Trinity. Paso of Christ of the Five Wounds.

On the former page, Nazarene of San Isidoro at the base of the Giralda.

renamed Nuestra Padre Jesús del Gran Poder (Our father Jesus from the Great Lord), which was opposed by Rome because it was not considered correct to refer to the second person in the Trinity as Father. Fortunately Seville triumphed and the Basilica is known by this same name with which the town recognises their Lord.

This life of the images is a trait of both Andalusia and Seville. There exists a devotion to them within other sectors of Christianity, naturally, but in few cases with this trait for the humanisation of the divinity (ever present in the lives and work of the people of Seville) and the deification of the humanity (which is cast and represented in the images). In spite of the fact that modern religious sensibility has to a great extent dispensed with the image as a fundamental element of worship, and that it is more than a century and a half has passed since Hegel wrote that "no purpose is served in finding the images of the Greek Gods magnificent and to see representations of God the Father, Christ and Mary: since we don't kneel before them" in the Catholic-Mediterranean Orbit, and in Seville in a very special way, thousands of people continually knelt before them, praying to them on a daily basis, carrying their photographs in their wallets and putting them in their homes and workplaces. This marks the difference. The vital and devotional link with the images has not debilitated over the last four hundred years in Seville. This demonstrates the undeniable fact that those which showed the greatest devotion were from the 17th century, with the Gran Poder (1620) and the Esperanza Macarena (probably at the end of this century) taking the lead.

Fathers register their sons with their brotherhoods barely before they are baptized, and don't waste any time doing so. They are dressed as Nazarenes whilst they are still infants. They are taken by the hand, throughout the year, to visit the images of their devotion in their churches. They are initiated into the mysteries of the pain and pleasure of Holy Week, carried to see the processions from being only a few months of age. They are brought closer firstly in arms, later to be lifted up so they can reach to kiss them at the annual *besamanos* (hand kissing) or *besapié* (feet kissing) ceremonies that each image has. In this way the devotion is handed down and they learn of Holy Week, in the same way they learn to speak, to walk, to recognize and to love. Many of Seville's infants' first recognitions include the face of the family's devotional image at the same time as that of their parents. Seville's theological chair is for these children, the arms of their parents as they point to the image of their devotion saying: "Look at the Lord". Parents in Seville know that their children are leaving infancy behind them when they are able to kiss the talon of the Gran Poder without the need to be lifted. The children learn all there is to know of what is signified by Sevillian devotion, to dress in a tunic and go out as a Nazarene when their fathers are shrouded in the gown from the brotherhood of their devotion, to learn of what the writer Sánchez del Arco called the definitive place of penitence which the entire members of Seville's brotherhood make before the Cristo de las Mieles, Jesus Christ in bronze which presides over the cemetery. And if the change of customs today extends to the incineration, the more truth there will to the saying, the flesh and the tunic melting in the same ashes worn on so many Holy Weeks by the Sevillian Nazarene.

This feeling of belonging to a tradition which is handed down as the greatest treasure and the splendid fundamental chaos which blends in with the street gatherings and its exaltation, joy and sorrow, respect and transgression are the most likely keys to understanding Holy Week. Not by way of an idealised literary elaboration or rhetorical topic, but the real intensity of this festival. As was demonstrated more than a century and a half ago, in 1849, when Holy Week was

Brotherhood of the Trinity.
Above, costaleros from the Sagrado Decreto.
Below, Nazarenes of the palio.

HOLY WEEK IN SEVILLE

The Hope of the Trinity.

adapted to a civic and romantic combination, the journalist and erudite Sevillian José Valázquez defined Holy Week as: The pious ceremony in which the arrogant great man, the elevated lady and the youthful gallant beau mix together in the house of God undistinguishable from the thug, the charming new Castilian, the Triana dweller and the young tender San Bernardo resident, giving exhibitions of this fervid religious spirit passed down from father to son as if it were the most precious heritage.

Nicea, the medieval Via Crucis, the splendour of the city's baroque enriched by gold from the Indies, the resurgence of the late romantic Seville and the Dukes of Monpensier, the regional customs of the twenties, all will be before the eyes of those who visit Holy Week in Seville, seen in images, on the floats, and within the creeds. But it is not to be forgotten that where the truth can best be seen is in the eyes of the people of Seville, a privileged mirror on their most profound secrets of love and of pain. Because Holy Week is a living celebration, which involves the most intimate of personal and family memories, the most protected of the consciences and their affects, but also in groups from districts and fraternities and the combination of a city which is both paralysed and mobilized in its entirety for a week. For this reason, this rich, complex and contradictory phenomenon has entered the 21st century laying the foundations of life as a personal, religious and sentimental experience; forming the backbone of the city as a group and collective experience; prompting goodwill through the fifty eight brotherhoods which actively unite a hundred thousand persons, imploring the intellectual and media

Brotherhood of the Holy Burial. «Triunfo de La Cruz» (Triumph of the Cross), know as «La Canina».

HOLY WEEK IN SEVILLE

world, to take a growing interest; promoting important modern charity and solidarity movements; and for all this, becoming the biggest religious movement in the Seville diocese.
At the worst so much vital exuberance is confusing to those unable to penetrate these mysteries of love since it does not allow them to penetrate, and the mixture of incense and smoke from churros (sweet fritters), of tears and joking, of silence and laughter, of gloomy streets with the passage of severe candle-lit black entourages and streets illuminated by bars replete with happy, noisy multitudes, makes you think that one of the two aspects is false. If there is so much happiness and the joy is so great, brightly, noisily and completely overflowing during the days of Holy Week, the profound emotion, the tears and the severity have to be pretence? If so many memories are wounded by this festival; if within it the hollow left by the dead is so sharply felt within the bustle, when we see the same brotherhood alone and in the same place in which we usually see it with some love that has been snatched away; if all this is so hard to bear, to the point where the gowns worn by the Nazarenes will be their shroud, the name of the image which accompanies them will be one of the last they speak and its face for them predicts the beauty of Paradise, could all the happiness be a transgression? This is not so. This is not Castile, and the greatest symbols of Holy Week the severe Gran Poder and the exultant Macarena are perfectly and marvellously represented only these extremes apparently irreconcilable. The key is that both are distinct forms of feeling and expressing the same: that the tenderness and suffering of

*Above, paso of the Holy Burial before the exit.
Below. The Piety of the Servitas.*

God (Gran Poder) has brought hope (Macarena) to mankind. How is it possible not to be distressed in the presence of the first and joyful in the presence of the second? And if devotion to them, as we see, is learnt as we learn to walk, to speak or to recognise those first dearly

*Virgin of Solitude.
Brotherhood of San Lorenzo.*

loved faces, how can we not manifest our joy or our sorrow, our happiness or our pain as we do in our everyday lives? Looking to my own memories, I recall what was the Virgin of Amargura in the calle Regina where I was born, the routine morning and evening visits to the church, the daily passing before her *azulejo,*(decorated tile) as if she was to reveal her mysteries and legends to the neighbours as if they were old family tales, her photograph presiding over the bedside tables and on the heads of cots in which so many of us the districts infants slept. How could they not have mixed misery and virtue, tears and laughter, baptisms and funerals within this frame of devotion woven around life with their own threads? The same could be said, in respect to the devotion between families or districts, of thousands of the people of Seville. The same is said today and they will say the same tomorrow of those being born in Seville, not only in its historic districts, but in the new: Tiro Línea, San Gonzalo, Nervión, Cerro del Águila, where there is no end to the birth of new brotherhoods, as distant as they may be from where these traditions were born they are able to continue speaking with God in the language of Seville.

The most magnificent aspect of Holy Week, the truly surprising and singular, is its capacity to express its content, vital and religious, as visual as it is sensual, in such a way that all those who take part, or truly know how to contemplate the event with the emotional sincerity that aesthetic communication

HOLY WEEK IN SEVILLE

demands, "to sense" for oneself, rather than try to understand the nucleus of the mysteries of religion and the human drama with which it is celebrated. For this reason, this festival is, at the same time and in a manner absolute, an experience both religious and humane. An experience which is preserved in life thanks to the devotion of the people of Seville, to the love of the devout and to the tenacity of the brothers who have maintained the brotherhoods for centuries with only the resources that they themselves make an effort to procure and with only the power of their love. These, the devout, the brothers and the brotherhoods are the most important part of Holy Week, after their devotion to the images: the togetherness, the affectionate encounter between these friends and acquaintances which are only seen here, the usual personal and family devotion to the images becomes communal to be tenderly and modestly shared with others, almost without speaking, these devotions so deep and intimate. Because it is the devotion to our images and the affection towards our brotherhoods, which unites us in the chapel, in the house of the brotherhood or in the bars where the people of Seville like to see us to speak of a thousand things about life, amongst which, as a part of it, are the brotherhoods and fraternities. Perhaps this is the most splendid aspect of the brotherhoods, being what makes them so humane, so much like flesh and blood. The loveliest and most moving aspect of Seville's Holy Week is to turn these works and this daily adoration into the city's grandest celebration, in such away that, rather than it being a suspension of everyday life, it is a glorification; not something given to the people of Seville done and paid by the powers that be, but which they do with their own efforts, in their great numbers and with their own hands. It is the city's fiesta par excellence because the city itself, as if it were an astonishing collective work of art and a proclamation born of a thousands hearts to be simultaneously proclaimed by a thousand voices, the creation, the living and the feeling.

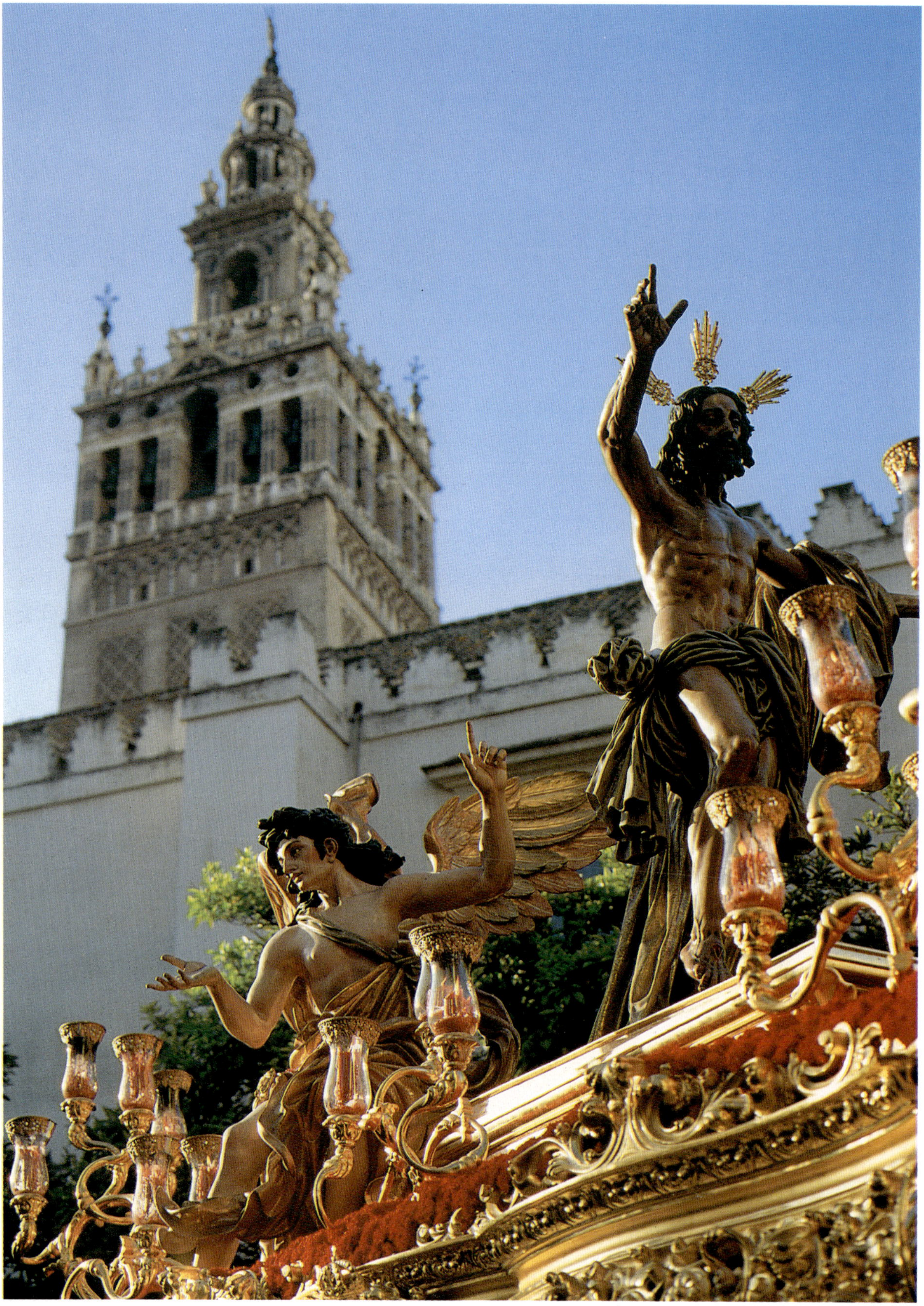